Dave & Carolyn

+ I wish you the Best in all that you do. You have been great friends

Marty Brickell

I Wish You Heavy Loads

by

Marty RicKard

© 2004 by Marty RicKard. All rights reserved.

No part of this book may be reproduced, stored in a retrieval system, or transmitted by any means, electronic, mechanical, photocopying, recording, or otherwise, without written permission from the author.

First published by AuthorHouse 04/07/04

ISBN: 1-4184-1371-2 (e-book)
ISBN: 1-4184-1374-7 (Paperback)
ISBN: 1-4184-1372-0 (Dust Jacket)

Library of Congress Control Number: 2004090787

Printed in the United States of America
Bloomington, IN

This book is printed on acid free paper.

For Whitney, Hannah and Luke Banker. Wow, wow and wow!
The entire earth should be populated by such angels

TABLE OF CONTENTS

A WISH FOR MY CHILDREN 1
TRUFFLES 3
MORE FOR MY CHILDREN 7
TATTERED PHOTOGRAPH 9
GONE 13
NAM 15
HAYING IN A DROUGHT 17
NEGATIVES 19
NATIONAL PASTTIME 21
IMPORTANT NUMBERS 23
SECRETS IN THE SKY 25
WINTER CLAWS 27
SNOWY STATUE 29
THE LINEBACKER 31
O'MALLEYS FIRST TIME 33
SWEET TEA 37
PROXIMITY 39
AWAKENING 41
PHOTOGRAPHER'S HELL 43
THE DRUNK NOVEMBER 45
LOST 47
THE CALL OF THE WOODS 49
EVERYTHING 51
THE AX 53
DIVERSITY 55
HEARTBEATS 57
WAITING FOR LUKE 59
BITTER BONES 61
WORD PONDERINGS 63
PROBLEM SOLVED 69

A WISH FOR MY CHILDREN

The world bristles with those
anxious to carry a light pack
on a wide path
down the hill
with a wind
at their back
that's never ill

I wish you heavy loads
on an up-grade
into a strong wind
on a virgin path
that takes some breaking
so you can inhale the joy of making
your own way through obstacles
that are not too few
and I pray your biggest barrier
shall not be you

Why do I wish you heavy loads
You must surely know
Steel that feels the fire
grows strong

And because I love you so

TRUFFLES

The infant sleeps in brittle arms
a creamy loaf
of mother's fresh bread dough
ready for the oven
of gluttonous years

My mind revisits my own youth
the time of the big war
the one to end them all
when Elms made tunnels
of pea-gravel streets
and camouflaged our virgin spirit
though it flourished like ivy on a stucco wall
in a wet spring

We fought our own war
and our enemy left us crippled
—if we were lucky

Our X-box
was a one-legged stick of a man
with liver lips and blotchy
brittle hands
propped on a creaky throne outside the tavern

He sucked a gurgling pipe
and
while we balanced our Schwinns
he blew out
through his smoke

stories of yet an older war
the one that took his leg

And he told us
about the trenches
and mud
the barbed wire
and blood
the fire
he felt
when he was shot

Sometimes
he cried
when he told
about his leg
lying next to him
in foreign mud

We glanced
at each other
How should
a child
react
to an old soldier's
tears

We looked
at the sidewalk
counted the cracks
and balanced
our Schwinns

more precisely

Would we
ever cry
like that
when we were old

One day he was gone
Only his hickory crutch
remained
a gnarled cross
slanted against lonely brick

It happens to everyone
our elders said
Even the creamy ones
grow up and die

But don't
—they warned
despair at truth
Seek the journey's rapture

My joy was creation
—rooting like a pig
in a pasture of words
seeking truffles

And when it ends for one
there comes another
Warm and white
bread dough

stuck to mother's breast
for a second
then baked to wrinkles
in the oven
of gluttonous years

And so it is
with words
When one
is used up
there is always
another
—always

But only
the truffles
survive

Only
the
truffles

MORE FOR MY CHILDREN

Tread strongly
on life's fickle road
I wish you power
your load to bear
Let friendship help you ease the pain
Waste not one second
on despair

A friendship forsaken
A path not yet taken
The most loving words
are left
unspoken
The greatest grace
is a promise unbroken

There's a difference between
being beat and beaten
done and finished
winning and being a winner
being a parent
and
being a father
or mother

There's a difference between
broke and broken
There's a difference between
a gentle word said
and a harsh word unspoken

But the greatest sin
is withholding yourself
from what might have been

TATTERED PHOTOGRAPH

She sat before me
wrinkled
gray
a tear upon her cheek
Her head was bowed
her eyes cast down
she could barely speak

Her husband of half a century
had taken glory's path
now all she had were memories
and one tattered photograph

She looked up with beggar's eyes
and asked so tenderly
Can you repair this photograph
It means the world to me

For fifty years I felt his touch
now death's torn us apart
This photograph is all I have
to ease my aching heart

I fixed the cracks across his face
and brightened up his eye
and when she saw the photograph
she could only cry

How much
she sobbed

It matters not
I'll pay any fee

I only want a smile
I said
That's good enough for me

She squeezed my hand
and paid her bill
and in a solemn tone
she said
my husband's picture
is the dearest thing I own

The months slipped by so swiftly
I saw her now and then
and every time
she took my hand
and paid her bill again

Then one day
she passed away
and I went to say goodbye
but when I saw her lying there
I couldn't help but cry

A gentle smile adorned her lips
and on her lifeless breast
they had placed that precious photograph
—it was her last request

Stocks and bonds and diamond rings

she left to fade away
She only took
the dearest thing
on that final day

Yes
she took that portrait with her
into eternity
and with that special photograph
went a tiny part of me

And each of us must ne'er forget
who share this precious craft
that wondrous thread of golden love
we weave into each photograph

GONE

Poor Tan is gone
Poor Tan is gone
away like leaves
in an autumn breeze

He was born black
on an old hay rack
We loved to run
in the prairie sun

He barked in fright
in the middle of the night
and when I awoke
he was gone

The thirteen years
he shadowed me
are painted
in my memory

But when I awoke
he was gone

NAM

Flesh dripped off like melting wax
and wailing trailed the thunder
What infant God hath put together
let no bomb tear asunder

An oranged cinchona skeleton
sang to a stormy moon
a song I never understood
from a ludicrous cartoon

Where was mother on the night
the stench vanquished my brain
and love was rape
in icy heat
and loving was profane

I saw those quaint and distant lands
where beneath a creeping pall
we spewed our half-breed semen
then tried to kill them all

Then they flushed us
down that toilet
as we hobbled home and found
a tormented
screaming cesspool
and the lucky weren't around

Home was another battlefield
where everyone's the enemy

and the only one who understood
was another lonely refugee
And the refugees
were you and me

Our haunting war has just begun
a fight for our humanity
Yes
our war has just begun
another stab at sanity

HAYING IN A DROUGHT

The metal monster growls
within the rows
eating miles of skimpy hay
and yielding little

And
on a quaking wagon
just behind
stand I
awaiting with reluctance
every dusty bale
Coughing up the chaff
as if it were a part
of me
and spraying spittle

And all
the while
the dreams
of eons
flow
from
my sweating soul
and stain
the ancient wood
by wear
made smooth
by time
made brittle

NEGATIVES

On the plains of the horizon
bleached in life's dying sun
lie the bones of thousands
who at the moment of decision
cried
IT CAN'T BE DONE

NATIONAL PASTTIME

Blame the food
for the fat
Blame the bar
for the inebriation
Blame tobacco
for the cancer
Blame the cheese
for constipation
Blame the car
for the accident
Blame the tree
for the paper torn
Blame the trooper
for the ticket
Blame the fence
for the picket
Blame
blame
America's favorite game
Blame the gun
for the crime
Blame the clock
if we're not on time
Blame
blame
that's our game
Blame Wal-Mart
if we fall
Blame is just
the American stall

and never solves
any problems at all
Responsibility
solves problems
Blame
is our clearinghouse
If you screw up
have no fear
blame someone else
you're in the clear
Blame McDonalds
for the coffee spill
If its hot
it's worth a mill
if it's not
we blame them still
return the swill
They blame the pot
and it costs us naught
Blame
blame
America's
favorite
game

IMPORTANT NUMBERS

How many people in China
Must be at least four billion
and each one
has two bicycles
which certainly
is not a crime-a
but they were all
in Kunming
at one time-a

SECRETS IN THE SKY

The wind churns through a sky of slate
Where're it goes it must be late
for some uncharted destiny
somewhere near eternity

My mother loved a stormy sky
and often I would see her weep
a silent tear
and she told me why
but made me promise
I would keep
the secret locked within my heart
a secret that I know so well
but can not tell

Mother's gone
but a roiling sky
reminds me of the times she'd cry
Reminds me of the reason why
Of a secret that still haunts me so
One that you can never know

WINTER CLAWS

Brittle cornstalks
lend a dusky murmur
to the timid
tenor voice
of autumn's chill

The language can't be understood
but if it could
it would reveal the autumn things I feel

The dying sun
each day
tucks itself away
beneath a lumpy quilt of sod
stitched by God

And how in haste
to race the dark
I gather eggs from hens
who shiver bony legs
into their straw-laced dens

As long as I'm able
I shall remember
the soups of September
at my mother's warm table

And summer flees
with passion
the winter claws

that
Lurk retracted
in the ashen paws
of brawling skies

Autumn conceives
such transcendent leaves
then shrouds in her breath their colorful death

And as another autumn falls
and is recorded
on forever's hallowed walls

the stalk
the sod
the leaf
we know
will seek their solace in the silent snow

The hills will sleep
the willows weep
and one year
closer to mortality
doth the reaper grimly creep

And now a silent voice within
begs a painful question
—Will I see this all again

SNOWY STATUE

Ice sickles dangle
from my nose
my fingers sting
how numb my toes

My ears are crisp
my ass is froze
and up my back
the wind she blows

But through it all
I love the snow
Now you must surely
want to know
why I like it when it snows
That reason I shall now disclose

You'll think it silly
I suppose
why I prefer
the snowy pose
Well
though the snow
adds to my woes
it hides the bird poop
on my clothes

THE LINEBACKER

He made Rambo Look
like a timid nun
'till his knee went out
now he's not
much fun

I never played football
like my brother
Howard
'cause I was
a little bit small
and quite a bit
coward

O'MALLEYS FIRST TIME

O'Malley tipped the bottle up
to slay his inhibition
to starch his spineless spine
for that sinful expedition

Then young O'Malley stalked the street
in vinyl shoes and sharkskin mist
above the beaconed phallic poles
the slimy concrete heaven-kissed

But floating in the pools below
the dregs converged in rosy turn
and the walls they shouted
no
no
no
and O'Malleys guts began to churn

Against the jellied stomach flood
that haunted him at every gate
years of silent status quo
clawed at such a sterile fate

The leg was long the ankle thin
and flames consumed the gate within
and O'Malley's brain took a crimson spin
and his pulse pumped in prelude to sin

With Wall Street speed and sheer delight
not one drip of negotiation

a bargain sealed in artic fright
and equatorial anticipation

A freckled sheet a flashing sign
The sister's kiss of tepid wine
And sweaty branches did entwine
in glee somewhat sub sublime

In a ninety-second's psychic smog
the flames devoured the willow log
and the eyes rolled back like a scalded dog
and sparks flew off in weightless fog

The mild meperidine delight
shattered by the vocal spear
flew off on soggy pigeon wings
The sigh was cast
'twas hora de ir

Not oft did mercy cloud her veins
but a twenty fluttered to the floor
Change
she smiled
for his lightning speed
and the honor of a righteous chore

Left in the silent flashing womb
of grey and green and withered bloom
O'Malley pondered his deplume
'gainst echoes from the locker room

The leg was long the ankle thin

this girl who carved his notch in fame
O'Malley picked the twenty up
He didn't even know her name

He'd fix it in the story told
change the sign to flashing gold
of soiled sheet he would withhold
and pick a name both kind and bold

The hated nervous anticipation
the vinyl sharkskin motivation
the spike-heeled inspiration
all better than the consummation

He stumbled down the gelded street
the path of sullied vinyl feet
and memories so bittersweet
his expedition now complete

SWEET TEA

Death lurks
at the bottom
of every cup
but between the lips
and those final sips
there is the sweetest tea
and we must never fear
to drink it up

PROXIMITY

Thousands die in distant lands
and we do not shed a tear
But
oh how long and hard we weep
when a loved one passes here

AWAKENING

A noisy dawn
unlocks
the chains of sleep
that bind me
to my bed

I must get up
I've chores to do
ideas to be fed
a poem
to write
for you

PHOTOGRAPHER'S HELL

When you feel that final tug
of the devil's awesome power
Hell won't be a lake of fire
but a wedding every hour

And from your lab most every day
where Hell's worst are employed
you get a call
and a fiendish voice
says
your film was all destroyed

But don't worry
laughs the person
in a tone that chills your spine
The amateur who shadowed you
Well
His film came out just fine

No one wants their picture took
and when they do they blink
but it doesn't really matter
cause your camera's not in synch

But two things down below
are like they were on earth
Cameras fall apart each week
and repairmen's fees exceed their worth

But all's not lost in Hades

I Wish You Heavy Loads

There's reason to give cheer
Your competitor didn't come
but all your friends are here

THE DRUNK NOVEMBER

The shredded pulp of memory
quivers through the glass
that hugs the wine so dearly
and hastens sense to pass
along life's solemn shaft
where feet melt swiftly on the path
that funnel of conformity
where vintage minds are gaffed

And every flower is red and green
and authority is most unclean
and ravens rap upon the door
and sanity shrieks
nevermore

Our bandaged minds are recompense
for all we're taught of common sense
and sex and horror are a bond
of all that we consider fond

And fire and ice are both a vice
and reality a pawn
that hides within the shriveled grass
and the soot that settles on the lawn

The Fish strain in a thickening sea
as genius hums its hollow tune
Hey
diddle
diddle

the cat ate the fiddle
while the men played on the moon

And amber waves engulf us
across the fruited plain
where atoms sell like apples
and the buyers are insane

And macho is insanity and
and manhood is profanity
and seconds are eternal
and nature is condemned

The dimming light our only strength
the faint light of creation
the essence of all life
the mushroom of salvation

One light will chain our souls
the other set us free
That blackened path least traveled by
or blessed purity

LOST

I lost a treasure
years ago
or
did it
lose me
We'll never know

It's odd
how something
lost for years
beneath the lonely
stars above
can summon up
such painful tears

THE CALL OF THE WOODS

The woods are soft
and etched with snow
They call to me
but I can't go

I must hurry to my work
For only boys play in the snow
Yes
I must hurry to my work
but to the woods my heart shall go

And in the woods my heart shall stay
until my final winter falls
Then lay me there beneath the oak
to answer when the forest calls

EVERYTHING

She stole my heart
and ran away
My dream of love
gone astray

Lonely years
in shades of blue
haunting tears
wanting you

Cast your image
from my sleep
and understand
me when I weep

I'm just a man
and it's from you
I get my strength
and weakness
too

I dry the silence
from my eye
Now at last
my heart can sing
for I see you
in everything

THE AX

From noisy liars
in noisy lairs
beneath the social sod
bony fingers flail the air like winter weeds
and clatter in the brittle breeze
confounding wants with needs

Toss a man a fish
feed him for a day
but teach a fish
to be a man
and revolution's on the way

They swim in sullen
frozen thought
while bloated bodies
on the hill
bathe in gold
and talk
and talk
and talk
and wonder why
oh why
when they lift them out
they die

Stand back and let them fly in flocks of one
on wings of wax too near the sun
so blistered eyes can search the earth

and find the spirit
where abounds the dearth

Give a man some milk
you feed him for a day
but when he owns the cow
he'll find a way
to get the hay

We must choose in life's deep woods
to gather nuts and tote them to the pens
or lead the swine to the pleasure 'neath the tree
to feed themselves
and set us free

Philanthropy's rope must be short
lest the quicksand claim the victim
before the slack is drawn
and the spirit drowns
of reason gone
awry

Don't wheel me down a beaten path
and to others give my load
No
Provide the ax
show me the woods
and let me clear my road

DIVERSITY

Diversity should be
the grain
of strong wood
and not
cheap veneer
which separates

Laminated wood
is strong
but the layers
are weak
Polish our wood
Don't peel layers

Multi-culturalism
is anti-patriotic
A coward's attempt
not to offend
anyone
which instead
offends all

No one wins
or loses
Everyone
is on one level

If all games
are tied
—why play

Nothing can be placed
above the other
for fear
that feelings
are hurt
How can we raise
our flag over another
Patriotism takes courage
Damned the cowardice
We are Americans
We *are* better
We are one wood
beautifully grained

I raise my flag proudly

If choosing my country
with all its layers
above all others
is politically incorrect
I am joyously that

Diversity
is grain
not veneer
It doesn't
need
to be taught
nor divided
Only cherished

HEARTBEATS

Let us always
keep a secret place
where we go often
to command
the energy of the ages
down upon us
like a fallen tent
of lace
in which two hearts
shall beat as one
Let us mold that cadence
into angels
who exist
to cherish our love

WAITING FOR LUKE

Two angels walk hand-in-hand
their tracks of laughter
grace the sand
One a lovely flowering rose
with music
in her nimble fingers
Shadowed by a daffodil
with prancing sunlight in her hair
and eyes
of such a crystal blue
so as to make the ocean sigh
that it might have
such color
too

Free from bonds of discontent
and pressures from above
they pause
beside the wrinkled sea
and listen patiently
to voices in a seashell
that inspire a fantasy

And though the sky be pewter grey
the sunshine of admiring glances
bathes them as they stray
to harvest shells for their tomorrow
and sprinkle joy on aging sorrow

They pause beside the salt-foamed sea

hold a seashell to the sky
listen to the seagulls cry
and wait impatiently
for one more dream
unseen
sailing the ocean
of the Amnion
on the crest
of the horizon
And soon there will be three

BITTER BONES

You are gone
Replaced by
the thick ropes
of bitterness
which hang
like curtains
in the darkness
of my anguish

Pewter castings
grown cold
fall from
a broken mold
of flesh
and sand
and dirty water
to crush your
tacit ambivalence
like flies
beneath the swatter

Frozen light
hindsight
tickles the dust
that dances
in the silence
of my weeping

I will watch the dust
gravitate

on invisible wings
and when each fleck
is considered
I will flee
before the maggots
swarm my dying soul
—leaving only
bones embittered

WORD PONDERINGS

Best a right word
moving like a snail
than a wrong word
too soon from the gate

Words can sting
or
cloud the way
Some are best
left unsaid
until they die
and
then decay

A word left unspoken
seldom hurts
But sometimes a word
that's never said can be
the worst you do

A promise unsaid
Is never broken
only the heart
that yearns to hear it

Words forged slowly
in the fire of thought
seldom go where
they ought not

I Wish You Heavy Loads

Words released
without thought
can harm
buy a farm
change a life
acquire a wife
bring strife

Words that live
only
in the heart
must be
good
and true
For words you lock
inside yourself
are only
heard by you

Some words
are worth
a thousand pictures

Words that hover
over sugar
like frenzied flies
are brittle
Words too sweet
attract only lies
buzz much
say little

Wrong words are bad
Bad words are wrong
Never use a weak word
when you can use a strong

Pleasure
pain
if in doubt
leave it out
A word should
say what it means
and mean what it says

True friends
never
bring bad words
to true friends

A simple word
that hits the mark
is better
than a thousand
gone astray

Words
like birds
can fly
where they
aren't wanted
Fences can't be built
around them

Birds
can be stopped
by nets
but nets can't stop
words
Words go where ere
the sound takes them
or the eye reads them
and are stopped
only by exhaustion
or louder words

Loud words
may go far
and say nothing
A whisper
can fall
at your feet
but say
the world

Curses advertise
brainlessness
Brainless words
are a curse

Words are short
Words are tall
Words can hate
or love
Fit like thorns
or like a glove

filet like a knife
cloud a sky
Sit on your heart
like a butterfly

Stones crumble
Mountains tumble
Words
withstand
it all

But sometimes
when one's in need
a deed
is better
than an ocean
of words

Words are wind
that turn the pages
Deeds are treasures
through the ages
Words are water
deeds are gold

But the greatest
of all these things
is love

PROBLEM SOLVED

I complained
because I had
no gloves

Until I met
a man
who had
no hands

So I took
his gloves

He screamed

There was
no need
for me
to run

Because
he couldn't
dial 911

About The Author

At age fourteen Marty RicKard moved to an old parsonage in the country. It was here that his passion for writing developed—and it was a dangerous passion. Iowa farm boys were expected to create muscles, not poetry.

Hard farm work put meat on his bones, and he learned to put sinew in his stories and poems—all the while hiding his writing from everyone. But one day he was caught. Someone found a poem in his jeans that he had forgotten to flush. (Read '**Hiding Clouds**' in Marty RicKard's book **"Sins From The Parsonage Window"**).

He was voted most likely to go to prison by his high school graduating class because of his fighting. He was a tough guy with the gentle heart of a poet. And an internal battle raged between those images as a teenager. Even in the Army he was forced into the boxing ring against his will.

RicKard survived, went on to earn a BS Degree in journalism from Southern Mississippi and then worked at the Oskaloosa Herald, Charles City Press, Mason City Globe-Gazette, Davenport Times-Democrat and was a technical writer for White Motor Company. As owner of the New Sharon Star, he twice was named Iowa Master Columnist for his weekly syndicated article.

He also owned an award-winning photography studio, and for eleven years wrote a column for Professional Photographer magazine. He has been published in many other magazines and newspapers, including Golf Digest, Resource Magazine, Picture, Range Finder, and Darkroom. He has won numerous photography awards, and has traveled internationally as teacher and judge.

Marty RicKard currently writes for Lens Magazine and the Fort Dodge (Iowa) Messenger. He also is a full-time writer of fiction and poetry. He is an entertaining and inspirational speaker and lecturer who always leaves his audience laughing. He can be reached at mrickard@iowatelecom.net" Other books by Marty RicKard are: ***Sins From The Parsonage Window***, and ***The Bony Fist Of Time.***

NOTES

NOTES

NOTES

NOTES

NOTES

NOTES

NOTES

NOTES

NOTES

NOTES

NOTES

NOTES

NOTES

NOTES

NOTES

NOTES

NOTES

NOTES

NOTES

NOTES

NOTES

NOTES

NOTES

NOTES

NOTES

NOTES

NOTES

NOTES

NOTES

NOTES

NOTES

Printed in the United States
21019LVS00001B/31-126